The Nativity Letters

by Nick Warburton

NCEC   RADIUS

No performance of this play may be given without the written permission of the publisher to whom all applications for performing rights should be made, enclosing a reply paid envelope.

The performance time is approximately 40 minutes

Published by:
National Christian Education Council
Robert Denholm House
Nutfield
Redhill RH1 4HW

Published by
RADIUS
Christ Church and Upton Chapel
Kennington Road
London SE1 7QP

British Library Cataloguing-in-Publication Data:
Warburton, Nick *1947–*
 The nativity letters
 I. Title II. National Christian Education Council
 822.914

 ISBN 0-7197-0724-2

A co-operative venture in Christian drama By NCEC and RADIUS

Series Editors: Sylvia Read and William Fry

RADIUS is the shortened name of the Religious Drama Society of Great Britain, bringing together amateur and professional actors, writers, and others involved in religion and the performing arts.

RADIUS exists to encourage all drama which throws light on the human condition especially through a Christian understanding. It aims to help local congregations to a deeper appreciation of all types of drama, to inform them of opportunities to see work of a high quality, to give the technical advice and assistance needed for a good standard of local productions, and to help them find ways of introducing the lively arts into their worship.

The Society runs a unique lending library, organises an annual summer school, holds regular play-writing competitions and publishes its own magazine.

First published 1990
© Nick Warburton 1990

All rights reserved. No part of this publication may be reproduced, stored in a retrieval system, or transmitted in any form, electronic, mechanical, photocopying, recording or other means without the prior permission of the publisher.

Typesetting by One and a Half Graphics, Redhill, Surrey
Printed by Halstan & Co. Ltd., Amersham, Buckinghamshire.

THE NATIVITY LETTERS

PRODUCTION NOTES

The action takes places in Nita's kitchen at home and also in the hall, classrooms and offices of her school. The stage is divided permanently into halves throughout the play to represent the locations of home and school.

Two tables are placed, one to left and one to right. The one on the left is Mrs Benson's desk with books, papers etc. The one on the right is Christine's kitchen table with knives, forks, jugs etc. At the back of the stage is a coat-stand for various props and bits of costume needed during the play.

DRAMATIS PERSONAE

CHRISTINE	(Nita's mother; fussy, old-fashioned, a little untidy)
NITA	(A strange girl; fourteen, cannot communicate)
TARRANT	(A youngish, idealistic teacher)
BENSON	(The Head; battle-weary, nervy)
TESS and EMMA	(Two girls at Nita's school)

THE NATIVITY LETTERS

A One Act Play

CHRISTINE sits writing at the kitchen table. NITA is slowly setting the table for breakfast.

MISS TARRANT stands at the desk, looking through a batch of envelopes and papers. MRS BENSON enters and puts her coat on the stand. The action in the kitchen freezes.

BENSON *(Sitting)* Morning, Meg. What brings you in here?

TARRANT *(Handing over some letters)* Mrs Allen asked me to give you these. This lot need dealing with today. *(Another batch)* These can wait.

BENSON *(Without enthuasiam)* Oh. Where is she?

TARRANT   Giving blood. She said the blood bank is entitled to a pint; the school can have the rest this afternoon. As usual.

BENSON   That woman thrives on moaning. *(Indicating the papers still in TARRANT'S hand)* What about those?

TARRANT   They have to be signed before they can be posted. Although, if you ask me . . .

BENSON   Which I didn't.

TARRANT   . . . most of them are unnecessary anyway.

BENSON   You're a teacher, Meg, not a secretary. You shouldn't have read them. Why are they unnecessary?

TARRANT   Are you asking me?

BENSON   I don't see what's unnecessary about them. I need to write them or the school won't run properly.

TARRANT   I don't know why you don't make more use of the 'phone.

BENSON   Because I am of the old school, that's why. A telephone conversation has no substance; you can't refer back to it. Besides, an epistle is more polite on the whole, don't you think?

TARRANT   Not when you have to type it out.

BENSON   You're beginning to sound like Mrs Allen's union rep.

TARRANT	But that's something I've noticed about you. You don't actually like talking to people.
BENSON	Haven't you got a class to go to?
TARRANT	That's really why you don't use the phone.
BENSON	I thought you said you didn't know why I don't use it.
TARRANT	Mrs Allen said if you sign them by nine they'll catch the second post.
BENSON	*(Looking at one of the envelopes)* Oh no, not Mrs Postan again. Has she nothing better to do than to write to me?
TARRANT	*(Going)* She's probably of the old school too.

MRS BENSON looks at the letter. Freeze.

The kitchen. CHRISTINE stands and turns to the audience.

CHRISTINE   Dear Mrs Benson, I was pleased when I first heard that Nita had to wear a uniform for her new school even though, in my position, it isn't easy to provide it. Now I am not so sure, though. Every day she comes home looking more untidy than she was when she left in the morning. What is the point of asking the children to wear uniforms and then ignoring their general appearance? It does seem as if there is no one at your school who is prepared to take proper note of the way children look. I am sure I am not the only parent concerned about these signs of slackness. I would appreciate your comments. Yours sincerely, Christine Postan.

MRS BENSON sighs and goes out. CHRISTINE turns back to the table where NITA is pouring milk onto a bowl of cereal. NITA stares as the milk trickles from the bowl to the table.

CHRISTINE   Nita!

Not quite immediately, NITA looks up.

What do you think you're doing? Look at this. *(Dabbing the milk up)* All you had to do was get the breakfast ready. A few cornflakes; simple enough. I can't leave you for a minute, can I? You're fourteen, Nita. Fourteen. You ought to be a help to me, not a hindrance. *(Pause while they*

	exchange looks) I sometimes think you do it on purpose.
NITA	Don't you want them, then?
CHRISTINE	Of course I don't! Not now. *(Slight pause)* It's 8.30. You'd better be going.

NITA moves slowly to the stand to get her blazer.

You know I like a proper table. All done nicely. You know I think that kind of thing's important.

As she finishes mopping up and returns to her writing, TESS and EMMA enter and take two chairs to centre stage. TARRANT enters and props herself on the edge of the desk. NITA puts on her blazer and hovers in the background.

EMMA *(Reading rather lifelessly from a book)* Yea, on a ley land,
I heard him blow: he comes here at hand
Not far.
Stand still.
TESS *(Also reading)* why?
EMMA Because he's coming, hope I.
TESS He'll tell us both a lie
Unless we beware.

She stops, having noticed NITA who has edged forward. MISS TARRANT looks up.

TARRANT	Yes? Nita, isn't it?
NITA	That's right, Miss.
TARRANT	Can I help you?
NITA	Pardon?
TARRANT	What do you want?
NITA	Can I join, Miss?
TARRANT	The Drama Club?
NITA	That's right, Miss.
TARRANT	Well . . . you've left it a bit late, haven't you?
NITA	I don't know. Have I?
TARRANT	We've been meeting all term. *(Pause)* We're just about to launch into something for the Christmas concert.
NITA	Oh. That'll be all right.

TARRANT	Why didn't you come earlier?
NITA	I want a bit of time to myself, you see, Miss.
TARRANT	Time to yourself?
NITA	That's right. From going home all the time.
TARRANT	I see. So you're not actually interested in drama.
NITA	I don't mind.
TARRANT	That's not really the point . . . Look, you're here now so you might as well join in for this week and we'll talk about it afterwards. All right?
NITA	All right.
TARRANT	We're reading from the Wakefield Shepherds' play. *(Handing her a book)* Here, you can read the Third Shepherd. Go back to the top of the page, Emma.

TESS and EMMA exchange glances.

TESS	Oh, Miss . . .
TARRANT	What?
TESS	Nothing, Miss.
EMMA	*(With a small sigh)* Yea, on a ley land,
	I heard him blow: he comes here at hand
	Not far.
	Stand still.
TESS	Why?
EMMA	Because he's coming, hope I.
TESS	He'll tell us both a lie
	Unless we beware.

NITA begins to read with a peculiar gusto that shocks the others.

NITA	Christ's cross me speed and St Nicholas!
	Of both I have need: it is worse than it ever was.
	We should take no need of the world, let it pass –
	This world never fared so
	Full of freaks as it does now . . .

She has risen and feels the eyes of the others on her. She turns to them. Freeze. TESS steps forward.

TESS	Dear Emma, If Nita Postan joins the Drama Club I think I'll leave. I can't help it but she gives me the creeps. You

never know what she's going to do next and, anyway, whatever she's involved in is mucked up for everyone else. If I leave will you leave too? Love Tess.

She leaves, followed by EMMA. NITA is about to leave too when TARRANT calls her back.

TARRANT	Nita.
NITA	Yes?
TARRANT	Do you still want to join?
NITA	If you like.
TARRANT	No, not if I like. Is it what you want?
NITA	I suppose so.
TARRANT	Come back here a moment. *(She waits for NITA)* You can join us if you really want to. If you're prepared to put in the work. *(Silence)* Is everything all right?
NITA	Yes thank you, Miss.
TARRANT	If there's anything you'd like to talk about . . .
NITA	Like what?
TARRANT	I don't know. Anything that's worrying you. That's partly why I'm here, you know.
NITA	Thank you, Miss. Can I go now?
TARRANT	Yes. Yes, of course.
NITA	I have to get to the Post Office, see.

She hangs her blazer on the stand and picks up a parcel. TARRANT watches her before she goes off.

CHRISTINE *(Looking up as NITA approaches)* Have you got it?
NITA   Yes.
CHRISTINE *(Taking the parcel)* Did they say anything? At the Post Office?
NITA   They just handed it over. They didn't ask any questions.
CHRISTINE   Well, why should they? I couldn't collect it so I sent you. What's wrong with that?
NITA *(Sitting and taking out a copy of the Wakefield play)* Nothing.
CHRISTINE *(Undoing the parcel)* Don't you want to know what it is?
NITA   If you like.
CHRISTINE   It's Christmas cards. I sent away for them. All different

	sorts. Four dozen. Look . . . a robin . . . stagecoach . . . Mary . . . *(NITA looks but says nothing)* It's not too soon, you know. Each one has to have a special message written for it. I don't believe in just signing them and sending them off. It all takes time. Nita?
NITA	Yes?
CHRISTINE	Would you like some?
NITA	What for?
CHRISTINE	What for? To send to friends of course, what do you think?
NITA	No.
CHRISTINE	You are lazy. Two or three wouldn't take you very long.
NITA	I don't want any.
CHRISTINE	You don't want any, what?
NITA	Thank you.
CHRISTINE	You'll feel bad. When you get cards and you haven't sent any.
NITA	I don't mind.
CHRISTINE	So there weren't any problems, then? *(Pause)* Only you were a lot longer than I thought. I was beginning to wonder . . .
NITA	I was late at school.
CHRISTINE	Were you? What, kept in?
NITA	No. Drama Club.
CHRISTINE	What?
NITA	Drama Club.
CHRISTINE	You don't have to stay for that, do you? I mean they can't make you stay, can they?
NITA	I suppose not.
CHRISTINE	Then you *want* to stay, do you?
NITA	They're doing a play for Christmas. Miss Tarrant said I could be in it.
CHRISTINE	Miss Tarrant said. *I'll* say if you can be in it, Nita. *(Pause)* I think you ought to take the cleaner upstairs, don't you? Make a start. All this staying around for plays has put you behind.

NITA goes. CHRISTINE turns to the audience.

Dear Jack, Anita is growing so fast these days. You'd be surprised. At times she seems so grown up. In fact, I don't think you'd know her if you saw her now. She likes her new school and is getting on well. She's very conscientious about homework and spends ages over it. Last week she joined the Drama Club. I can't really imagine her doing plays and things. She says she's going to be Mary in a thing they're doing for Christmas. We still get on together and she makes herself very helpful about the house. All the same, I'm sure she'd love to see you again and perhaps you ought to make time for a visit. I know your work is important and it must be difficult to get away but aren't we important too? Could you be back for Christmas, do you think? Please be in touch again soon. As always, my love, Chris.

She returns to sorting her cards.

BENSON and TARRANT enter, BENSON sitting at the desk.

BENSON   She reads well enough. She can write. She understands most of what we say to her.
TARRANT   Yes, and she's disruptive.
BENSON   No, Meg, she's not. Not in any quantifiable sense.
TARRANT   What would you call it, then?
BENSON   I'd say she was . . . odd.
TARRANT   Odd? But what's the difference when it comes down to it?
BENSON   She's not like the others, I know, but it doesn't follow that she's disruptive. Odd isn't necessarily disruptive.
TARRANT   Maybe not, but odd is odd and in itself may mean she needs help.
BENSON   What sort of help, Meg?
TARRANT   I don't know.
BENSON   When I started teaching they would have said she was potty and left it at that. And she'll probably grow up to be a potty adult . . . eccentric if you prefer. There's not much you can do about it.
TARRANT   Yes . . . well, we understand things a bit better now.

BENSON	Do we? We've got a few more labels for things, that's all. And, anyway, maybe people should be allowed to remain odd. After all, it's only the occasional odd person who makes the rest of us seem normal, isn't it?
TARRANT	So you're saying we should do nothing?
BENSON	I'm saying there's little we can do.
TARRANT	And Nita's all right?
BENSON	Depending on what you mean by 'all right', yes. She's a bit uninhibited at times.
TARRANT	Oh, uninhibited now, is it?
BENSON	All children need to develop inhibitions: maturity is impossible without them. Nita's probably slow off the mark but she'll catch up.
TARRANT	I see.
BENSON	Of course, if there's anything you feel you can do to help you're welcome to try. Your efforts will be appreciated; by me if not by her.

TARRANT turns away and BENSON leaves. EMMA, TESS and NITA enter and take up positions in the centre in order to rehearse. NITA sits and the others stand either side of her. NITA stares blankly.

EMMA Hail! I kneel and cower. A bird have I brought to my dear.
Hail, little tiny mop,
Of our creed you are crop!
I would drink in your cup,
Little day-star.

She mimes giving a bird to NITA who takes no notice.

TESS Hail! Sweet is your cheer: my heart would bleed
To see you sit here in such poor need
With no pennies.

TARRANT You'll have to be louder than that, Tess. And for goodness' sake put more life into it.

TESS *(Louder)* Hail! Put out your hand small.
I bring thee but a ball
Have and play thee withal,
And go to the tennis.

	Again NITA does not respond to her mime. TESS sighs heavily.
TESS	It's no good, Miss Tarrant. She's never going to do this properly. Look at her . . .
	NITA snaps out of it and suddenly goes for TESS. There is a struggle and EMMA holds NITA off.
TARRANT	*(Intervening)* Nita! Nita! Stop that!
	Just as suddenly NITA stops. She goes limp as EMMA holds her. Emma detaches herself with some embarrassment.
TESS	What's the matter with her? I'm not going to do it if she stays in it.
TARRANT	All right, Tess. Calm down.
TESS	The stupid cow! You should chuck her out!
	TESS runs off.
TARRANT	Tess! *(To EMMA)* See if she's OK, will you?
	EMMA, glad to get out, follows TESS off. NITA slumps into the chair.
TARRANT	What was all that about?
NITA	Nothing.
TARRANT	I don't think Tess thought it was nothing.
NITA	Are you doing what she said? Am I chucked out?
TARRANT	I'll tell you if I want you to leave, Nita.
NITA	Maybe you should. Maybe I'm not good enough.
TARRANT	And if I didn't think you could do it I wouldn't have asked you to take the part.
NITA	But it's a laugh, really, isn't it? Me, Mary?
TARRANT	Look . . . I'm always in here at the end of the day. If you ever want a chat . . .
NITA	What for?
TARRANT	I don't know. I'm just saying, I'm here if you'd like to come. All right?
NITA	What about punishment?
TARRANT	I don't punish people for being upset.

NITA	Just conversation?
TARRANT	If you like.
NITA	I don't know.

NITA goes. TARRANT steps towards the audience. There is anger behind her letter.

TARRANT	Dear Mrs Postan, Would it be possible for you to come and discuss Anita's progress? I feel . . . I feel I am getting to know her and a consultation would be most productive at this stage. Yours sincerely, Margaret Tarrant.

BENSON enters.

BENSON	I suppose you realize there's rather a lot at stake.
TARRANT	Of course. There always is with productions. . . .
BENSON	I mean the hall is going to be packed for an occasion like this. Christmas is always the same.
TARRANT	Well?
BENSON	What are you going to do about Nita Postan?
TARRANT	What should I do?
BENSON	I'm worried about her, Meg.
TARRANT	Oh. *You're* worried.
BENSON	I know, I know. This probably seems like an about face to you . . .
TARRANT	It does rather, yes. You said there's nothing we could do about Nita. Now you're asking me what I plan to do . . .
BENSON	There's a difference between Nita in class and Nita under the glare of public scrutiny, on the school stage . . .
TARRANT	She won't let you down, Mrs Benson.
BENSON	You still intend to use her, then?
TARRANT	Why, do you intend to stop me?
BENSON	Of course I don't. You know that's not my way.
TARRANT	Then, yes, I intend to use her.
BENSON	As what?
TARRANT	Mary.
BENSON	Mary? Oh God!

TARRANT	She'll be all right.
BENSON	It's nice to hear you speak with such ringing confidence, Meg, but what's it going to look like if the Virgin Mary suddenly decides to beat up one of the shepherds in front of a hall full of parents? What's it going to look like for Nita? You must agree it would take the edge off the evening; not to say the whole festive season.
TARRANT	We've had a chat about that. It won't happen again.
BENSON	Are you sure?
TARRANT	In any case, I think it's important that we give her the chance . . .
BENSON	The risk is considerable. I suppose you realize that.
TARRANT	But necessary.
BENSON	Well, it's easy for you to say that — it makes you sound terribly caring and dedicated — but if Nita fouls up the evening by doing something silly it's me who'll get the blame. Much as I'd like to I won't be able to pass it all onto you.
TARRANT	If it worries you that much . . .
BENSON	All I'm saying is don't be wrong.

They exit.

The kitchen. Christine is writing, NITA preparing the table for a meal. NITA hesitates by CHRISTINE before slipping a couple of Christmas cards away. She turns to the audience.

NITA *(Holding up the first card)* To Emma, with fond memories for a Happy Christmas. From your friend, Nita Postan. *(The second card)* To . . . to . . . a happy Christmas to . . .

She struggles to think of someone else as CHRISTINE looks up.

CHRISTINE Nita? What're you doing?
NITA *(Hiding the cards)* Nothing.

CHRISTINE   Well, I thought you were supposed to be getting the tea ready.
NITA   That's what I was doing.
CHRISTINE   By gawping into space? We'll end up starving if that's how you manage things. *(Slight pause)* Did you take those things out to the shed?
NITA   Yes.
CHRISTINE   Because I can't. You know I can't. I have to depend on you.
NITA   I know.
CHRISTINE   You probably think that's your bad luck but it's not specially nice for me, you know. Having to be so dependant.
NITA   I've done them.
CHRISTINE   Good girl.

She stands and turns to the audience as NITA returns to the table.

CHRISTINE   Dear Miss Tarrant, I see no point in meeting to discuss Nita. I have no problems with her at home. If this is not the case at school I would suggest that you need to put your own house in order. The difficulties, if they exist, stem from a slackness at school. In any case, I am, at the moment, unable to come to the school. My doctor has advised me to stay in. Yours faithfully, Christine Postan.

She returns to the table.

The classroom. TARRANT enters reading this letter. As she finishes, she screws it up angrily and turns to the desk to pack away some books. NITA crosses to her and hesitates.

NITA   Miss Tarrant . . .
TARRANT *(Turning)* What?
NITA   You said . . .
TARRANT   Nita? Is that you?
NITA   Yes.
TARRANT   Come right in, then. So I can see you properly.
NITA *(Approaching)* You said to come. I . . . if I wanted to chat . . .

TARRANT   Yes. Of course.

A pause. Neither knows what to say next.

TARRANT   Well . . .
NITA   What?
TARRANT   What did you want to chat about?
NITA   I don't know. Just chat, I suppose.
TARRANT   Would you like to sit?
NITA   No. No, thanks.

She immediately begins to pace and wander.

TARRANT   Oh. Perhaps you'd just like to . . . wait, then. While I get ready.
NITA   Yes, if you like.
TARRANT   You always say that.
NITA   Do I?
TARRANT   Well, you say it a lot.
NITA   I never noticed.
TARRANT   Perhaps you feel a little awkward at the moment. It's not easy, just to launch into a chat, is it? *(Pause)* Perhaps next time you'll feel more like speaking. What do you think?

Freeze.

The kitchen. CHRISTINE has some of her cards.

CHRISTINE   To Ted and Milly, with best wishes for Christmas. It's such a long time since you came over to see us. Perhaps you'll be able to make it this year. There's a lot to catch up on. Love Christine and Anita. *(Another card)* To Dear Jack, with best wishes for Christmas. Well, it looks as if you won't make it back by Christmas. We keep hoping, though, of course. I'm sending this with the hope that it reaches you in time. Perhaps you could phone. I would be glad to talk about Nita. She spends more and more time at school and I'm not convinced that it is such a good influence. She says she is practising for a play but I wish I could be sure. She's just growing up, I suppose, but the evenings do seem long when she stays late. It would be nice to talk about it. You and me, I mean. As ever, all my love, Chris.

The classroom. Some days have passed.

TARRANT *(After a pause)* I really will have to go soon.
NITA That's all right.
TARRANT I have to go out tonight. Well, not *have* to, I suppose . . .
NITA I don't mind.
TARRANT Look, Nita. This is the third time you've come to see me after school . . .
NITA Do you want me to stop, then?
TARRANT Of course I don't. I said you could come, didn't I? But you don't talk. You don't say anything.
NITA I do.
TARRANT Hardly. Don't you trust me? Is that it?
NITA *(Looking at her, almost for the first time)* It's not that. It's just that it's hard.
TARRANT What's so hard about it?
NITA I'm not talking about having a chat. I'm talking about explaining things. That's what's hard.
TARRANT Shall I ask you questions, then? Would that help?
NITA If you like.
TARRANT *(Immediately)* How do you get on with the others?
NITA What others?
TARRANT You know what I mean.
NITA All right.
TARRANT Is that what you think? Because it doesn't look all right to me.
NITA Doesn't it?
TARRANT You never speak to them; and, on the whole, they ignore you.
NITA It doesn't bother me.
TARRANT Really? Doesn't it?
NITA Why should it? What difference does it make?
TARRANT A lot, I think. To you.

NITA	It's all right for you . . . *(She stops herself)*
TARRANT	What?
NITA	They like you. They all like you. *(Pause)* They have to pick on someone, don't they?
TARRANT	You?
NITA	That's what it looks like.
TARRANT	Why? I mean, why don't they like you?
NITA *(Angry)*	How should I know? I can't get inside their heads.
TARRANT	Don't you ever wonder about it?
NITA	What good would that do?
TARRANT *(After a pause)*	Does the play worry you?
NITA	Yes.
TARRANT	You don't have to do it, you know. I'm not making you.
NITA	You want me to drop out?
TARRANT	I didn't say that. You should only do it if you want to do it.
NITA	Well I do. I do want to do it.
TARRANT	Nita! That's the first time I've ever heard you say that. You really want to do something.
NITA	I suppose so.

For the first time she smiles. It is only then that we see that her last line is intended to be ironic. However, TARRANT'S next line destroys this mood.

TARRANT	Will your mother come?

CHRISTINE stands and looks towards NITA.

CHRISTINE	I *can't* come, Nita. Dr. Stock wouldn't allow it.
NITA *(Crossing from the classroom)*	Miss Tarrant asked.
CHRISTINE	Her? It's got nothing to do with her.
NITA	I suppose not.
CHRISTINE	What's she want to go sticking her nose in for?
NITA	She asked me to ask, that's all.
CHRISTINE	Then you know what you can tell her. Anyway, Nita, you don't want me to come, do you?
NITA *(Shrugs)*	It's up to you.

CHRISTINE *(Angry)* No, it isn't up to me! That's what I'm saying; can't you listen? *(Pause. NITA backs away a little. Then calmer)* It would be different if Dad was back in time but it looks as if he's not going to make it. So you won't mind, will you?
NITA I won't mind.
CHRISTINE And you'll have your friends. That's much better. I know I was always embarrassed when my Mum came up to the school. It'll be better for you to have your friends.

NITA turns away. CHRISTINE is stranded. She looks lost and hopeless. NITA takes out the card she wrote.

NITA To Emma, with fond memories for a happy Christmas. From your friend . . . your friend, Nita Postan.

Suddenly she rips the card up.

NITA *(To TARRANT)* Friends? How would she know? I'll tell you what it's like: I don't understand them and they don't understand me. I don't mean I don't know what they're like. I mean I don't know what they're *saying*.
TARRANT And do you understand me?
NITA You're different. I see them speaking. Their mouths move. The words come spinning out and then they change in mid-air, like clouds, and I don't know what they're supposed to mean any more.
TARRANT So you make mistakes.
NITA And I look like an idiot.
TARRANT Which you're not.
NITA Aren't I? I feel like one.
TARRANT And this is why you never speak to the others?
NITA It's just easier if I don't. Besides, I can see what they're thinking by the looks on their faces. Weirdo. Nutter. Freak.
TARRANT They're not all like that . . .
NITA I'm not saying they're wrong, Miss Tarrant.
TARRANT What about home? Your parents?
NITA Mum, you mean. Dad's gone.
TARRANT Yes, of course. He works away, doesn't he? Abroad somewhere . . .
NITA Works away? He's gone. I just told you.

TARRANT	But I thought . . .
NITA	That's what she says, I suppose, but it's not true. He's just gone. Left. More than a year ago.
TARRANT	Left?
NITA	You can't really blame him, can you. Couple of freaks like us . . .
TARRANT	I'm sorry, Nita. I didn't realize . . .

During the next speech TARRANT begins to move back and off, very slowly and not listening. NITA doesn't notice.

NITA   She writes to him, you know. At least once a week, even though she never gets an answer. I know because I have to post the letters and sometimes I open them up to see what she's said. It doesn't matter. They're not going to get to him, are they? She's not coming to the play. I know I don't have much to do but at least it's something. More than I've ever done before. At least people can't pretend that I don't exist, smirking behind their stupid hands all the time. It's no good telling me she can't help it. Of course she can help it. It suits her to stay in all day, on her fat backside with her pointless, bloody letters to people she never ever sees! Why did I have to get stuck with her? I hate her!

As she turns to find she is alone, CHRISTINE stands and leaves.

Miss Tarrant . . .? I'm sorry for shouting like that. I ought to be getting ready for the play, I suppose . . . Thank you for listening to me.

She is about to leave when BENSON, now very smart, ENTERS.

BENSON	Nita? What are you doing here?
NITA	Nothing.
BENSON	Aren't you supposed to be changed?
NITA	I'm just going. I was . . .
BENSON	What?
NITA	I was looking for Miss Tarrant.
BENSON	She hasn't arrived yet.

NITA	No.
BENSON	Hadn't you better be going?
NITA	I suppose so.
BENSON	Good luck with the play. You won't . . .
NITA	Won't what?
BENSON	You'll do your best? I'm sure you will.
NITA	Yes. I suppose so.

She goes and BENSON turns to the audience.

BENSON Dear parents, you are cordially invited to an evening of festive entertainment by the Lower School, at 7.30 on Thursday 18th December. The choir and orchestra will perform a number of pieces and the Drama Group will present an extract from the Wakefield Mystery Plays. Seats are limited and we can only accommodate those who fill in the reply slip and return it to us by Friday 12th. Yours sincerely, A.F. Benson *(Head).*

TARRANT, also smart, hurries on to join her.

TARRANT Sorry I'm late. The blessed car wouldn't start. Of all nights!
BENSON *(Indicating audience)* Look at them all, Meg. Sitting there all smart and expectant. It gives me the jitters.
TARRANT Why on earth should it do that?
BENSON It's too like the circus. Half the pleasure for some of this lot is in thinking that something will go wrong.
TARRANT Rubbish. Anyway, nothing will go wrong.
BENSON No? You wouldn't be so sure if you'd seen what I've just seen.
TARRANT What was that?
BENSON Nita Postan.
TARRANT Nita? She is here, then?
BENSON Meg, she was shouting her head off.
TARRANT What?
BENSON All by herself, in an empty room.
TARRANT Oh, no. Is she all right?
BENSON How should I know? Have you seen her?
TARRANT I haven't seen any of the kids. I ought to make sure there's nothing wrong, I suppose.

BENSON   Yes, I think you ought. As far as I can make out you're the only one she talks to.
TARRANT   Not really. She came to see me a couple of times but she would never speak. She's completely sealed off from everybody else.
BENSON   Well just do the best you can, will you . . .

> *She is interrupted by a banging at a door in the auditorium.*

          Now what?
TARRANT   Someone trying to get in by the looks of it.
BENSON   Oh, for God's sake.
TARRANT   What it is to be popular.
BENSON   They can't come in; it's far too late. Look, you go and sort Nita out. I'll see to this.

> *BENSON heads for the door in the auditorium and goes out that way. TARRANT goes out at the back of the stage. For a moment we hear the sound of girls singing a Christmas song. As it fades the three girls enter and take up positions: NITA seated between the other two who stand. They are dressed for the play.*

EMMA *(With more spirit than last time)* Hail! I kneel and cower. A bird have I brought to my dear.
Hail, little tiny mop,
Of our creed you are crop!
I would drink in your cup,
Little day-star.

> *She kneels and sets a small bird cage at NITA'S feet.*

TESS   Hail! Sweet is your cheer: my heart would bleed
To see you sit here in such poor need;
With no pennies.
Hail! Put out your hand small.
I bring thee but a ball,
Have and play thee withal,
And go to the tennis.

> *She kneels and proffers a ball. NITA, absently cradling a doll, ignores her. TESS panics slightly and waves the ball about a little.*

NITA *(Looking at her)* Why should I?
TESS   *(Hissing)* Take it!
NITA   What, from you?
TESS *(Desperate)* Please!

           NITA stands and, after an agonizing pause, takes it.

NITA   The Father of Heaven, God omnipotent,
That the world has given, his son has sent:
My name could he name even, and laughed as if he knew
   his father's intent:
I conceived him through God's might, even as He meant,
May he keep you from woe:
I shall pray him so,
Tell the world as you go,
And remember this morn.

           They freeze for a moment.

           CHRISTINE enters the kitchen and takes off her coat. The girls either side of NITA then leave.

CHRISTINE   Dear Miss Tarrant, I would like to know if the Christmas play went well for Nita. I tried to come because I could see what it meant to her. Perhaps you won't understand this, but I found it hard to leave the house. It was quite dark, though, and that helped. When I got to the school I couldn't get in — I don't know why; I think I hadn't told them I was coming or something. Anyway, I didn't know what to do and so I've come back here. I shouldn't be like this, I know. I realize that it isn't really your concern but I wonder if there is someone you know who might talk to me about it. At the moment Nita is not bringing her friends home and I'm afraid it may be partly my fault. I think they would come if it wasn't for me. Thanking you for what you've done for Nita, yours faithfully, Christine Postan.

           CHRISTINE and NITA are alone on the stage. They turn to look at each other.
           Fade lights.

           THE END